This is the second book about Brownies around the world, so you can find out about Brownies in eleven more countries including Canada. All these countries are members of the Guiding family, called The World Association of Girl Guides and Girl Scouts. This large family grew from the ideas and work of Robert Baden-Powell, and now there are Brownies, Guides and Rangers in nearly 100 countries of the world.

Robert Baden-Powell and his wife Olave, share the same birthday, February 22nd and many years ago, this day became known as Thinking Day, a day for circling the world with a chain of warm, friendly thoughts. Birthdays make us think of gifts, and one Thinking Day, a Guider in Belgium had an idea. "Wouldn't it be nice, if, on Thinking Day, we could each give one small coin to help some of those in Guiding who specially need our thoughts and help!" From this idea, came Thinking Day pennies and the World Friendship Fund.

Contents

Brownies Around the World

To the Brownies of Canada

ISBN 0-919220-03-7

This pin may be worn in or out of uniform by anyone who has made her Promise in any country which is a member of the World Association.

Canada

Canada is a very large country which stretches many hundreds of miles from the Atlantic to the Pacific Ocean and far up north to the Arctic. There are high snow-capped mountains, vast forests, beautiful lakes, large cities and towns as well as miles and miles of prairie and farmlands and rocky ocean coasts.

In this huge country there are many Brownie Packs. In the far north, there are Inuit Brownies who speak their own language. In some provinces, there are Indian Brownies in Packs on their own reservations or in residential schools where they are learning English. French speaking Roman Catholic Brownies belonging to the Guides Catholiques du Canada (secteur français) and called Jeannettes are found in eight provinces across Canada but mainly in the Province of Quebec, and English speaking Brownies are found everywhere across Canada.

A Brownie's uniform is a brown dress, a white tie with orange maple leaves on it, and brown shoes and socks. A Jeannette wears a blue skirt and light blue blouse with a yellow tie. Her stockings or knee length socks are blue.

Testwork for Brownies in Canada

Brownies in Canada are between the ages of 6 and 9 years. They earn their Golden Bar, Golden Ladder and Golden Hand badges. One of the favourite Golden Bar activities is to make a picture or object from seeds or other natural materials. For her Golden Hand, a Brownie may learn, under mother's care, how to use the stove in her own home. Then she may prepare and serve two different kinds of food, such as a cooked vegetable, or soup, or a salad or a cooked dessert, which may be cake or cookies, or prepare and pack a lunch to take on an outing.

A Brownie earning her Golden Hand Badge enjoys taking part in outings. She learns to look after herself in the outdoors, and how to use a compass. Jeannettes follow a programme to gather Blue, White and Gold Flower badges. They learn to gift-wrap a present for someone, and to write invitations to parties and thank you notes for gifts and visits. They also mime or act little plays. Jeannettes learn simple first aid for small injuries such as cuts and burns. They also learn to sew and embroider and knit; then they make a scarf or pot holder etc. to earn a badge.

Canadian Brownies like to work for Interest Badges, and there are thirty-six different ones. Two very popular ones are Housekeeper and Explorer. To become a Housekeeper, a Brownie learns with her mother how to sort clothes to be laundered, how to tidy, clean and dust a room, how to clean a bath, basin and refrigerator, how to fry bacon and egg and tidy up afterwards, and go on a shopping errand for mother.

To earn an Explorer badge, six Brownies at a time go exploring with Brown Owl or Tawny Owl. They plan together where to go, what to wear and what to take. On the trip, they carry their equipment (lunch, First Aid Kit, etc.) in haversacks on their backs and learn the use of a compass and simple map-making.

Good Turns

Canadian Brownies and Jeannettes like to do good turns, especially as a surprise. In many Packs, all the Brownies work together several times a year to help other people. At Christmas-time, gifts are made, Christmas stockings packed, and carols sung to children and old people who are in hospital at that time. Packs often give parties for under-privileged children and fill baskets with goodies to be delivered to handicapped people.

Brownies help with litter-chases to clean up the countryside. They also collect uniforms and help to make equipment for Brownie Packs in the far north, and in poorer parts of the large towns and cities.

Inuit Brownies often carry younger children of the family on their backs in special baby-carrying parkas. They help their mothers to chew sealskins so they are easier to sew.

Games Canadian Brownies Like to Play

"The Laughing Game"

Indian Brownies of British Columbia sent this game to be printed in this book. It is played in the Indian bands to teach control of features, a skill which is very important to Indians.

The Brownies sit in a circle with one who is "IT" in the centre. "IT" makes a funny gesture, or face, or sign, looks round quickly to see if anyone laughs or smiles, and tries to catch that Brownie by pointing to her. The Brownie then becomes "IT" for the next turn.

"The Fisherman"

Set out chairs in a square, facing inwards, but with openings at the four corners. The Brownies sit on the chairs, except for one who is the Fisherman and she stands outside the circle. Brown Owl has a list of many kinds of fish and she gives each Brownie (including the Fisherman) the name of a different fish.

The Fisherman then walks or runs gently round the outside of the square while Brown Owl calls out the names of about half a dozen fish to be caught. These Brownies get up, go out of the square at one of the corner openings, and follow the Fisherman. When the Brown Owl calls "Rod and Line", the Brownies outside continue in the same direction to the next opening and run in to sit on an empty chair (no one may change direction and run back). The Brownie left without a chair is the next Fisherman.

Games in the Far North

After the long winter darkness, the Brownies of the Arctic make the most of summer sun. They enjoy skipping, chasing and ball games. As the days get longer, children are often out playing at 1 or 2 o'clock in the morning. They sleep when they get tired! In times gone by, the Inuit children were required to play "Cat's Cradles" while the sun was disappearing in the fall, in order to prevent its disappearance!

Language

English and French are the official languages of Canada, but Indians and Inuit also speak their own languages.

English	French	MicMac	Inuktituk	Ojibway
Good day	Bon jour (bon joor)	Welygisgouk (It is a nice day)	Silasiak	Ahneen, boozhoo
Thank you	Merci (mair-see)	Welawlin	Kujannamik	Megwach
Good bye	Au revoir (Owe revwah)	Adieu	Tawawutit	Boozhoo, bambi qua-men (see you later)

9

The Story of the Totem Pole in Kitimaat

The Indian craftsman had found a fine piece of yellow cedar to be carved into a totem in honour of Canada's 100th birthday. He made it tell a legend of the people of his village and show the crests of the clans of Kitimaat.

The Beaver sits at the bottom, his tail in front; behind him is the Grizzly with a Salmon in his mouth. In the next section is the figure of Tahnees, a wild man who only appears at ceremonies to honour people of high rank like himself. He goes among the guests biting those he wishes to honour. The Frog is shown next on the totem and then Wee-git, the Raven, who can turn himself into any other creature. The Owl sits above Wee-git, with every feather delicately carved.

The next section tells the legend of a man named Sa-ga-dee-law. His wife was washing her robe of otter-skin when she was captured, and she is shown clinging to the back of a killer whale as she is carried away to the underwater world. Sa-ga-dee-law, with several men in his canoe, pursued them, and when he came to the place where the whale sounded, he made a long pole of cottonwood branches, sank one end to the sea-bottom and climbed down to rescue his wife.

The top of the totem is completed with figures of the Black Bear, the Frog and the Wolf, and on the very tip, the Eagle sits hunched forward just as he is often seen on tops of the tallest trees.

The totem made the long journey across Canada in 1967 to represent the people of Kitimaat during Expo and Canada's Centennial. Then it returned to Kitimaat Village where you may see the figures carved in its golden wood if you visit the Centennial Museum there.

Things to do

What could you do with this Indian legend? Draw the totem pole? Model it in plasticine? Tell the story to your Pack? Ask a few other Brownies to act with you the adventures of Sa-ga-dee-law?

In the eastern part of Canada, Brownies often go to the maple sugar bush in the spring to taste the maple syrup. See if you can find a book in a library and read how the trees are tapped, and the sap boiled to make a lovely golden syrup or sugar.

Canada's famous police force is called The Royal Canadian Mounted Police (the Mounties). They wear bright red coats when on parade. As well as riding horses, they now travel by car, motor cycle, motor boat, ship, plane, snow-mobile and dog-sled. See what else you can find out about them.

Canada has many beautiful National Parks such as Banff. Could you make a scrapbook with pictures of some of them?

Find a dime and look at the ship on it. She is called The Bluenose. Could you find out some more about her, and perhaps make a model or a drawing.

Learn a piece of Canadian poetry to say to your Pack. You might like "Indian Summer" by Wilfred Campbell, or "Something told the Wild Geese" by Rachel Field.

The Huron Carol

This Christmas Carol was specially written for the Huron Indians by Father Jean de Brébeuf, a French missionary. In 1642 he wrote:

'The Indians . . . built a small chapel of cedar and fir boughs in honour of the manger of the Infant Jesus . . . Even those who were at a distance of more than two days' journey met at a given place to sing hymns in honour of the new-born child.'

This is the version used now by English-speaking Canadians—although it was, of course, first written in the Huron language. Notice how Father Jean de Brébeuf has used ideas that the Indians themselves were familiar with to tell the story of the birth of Christ.

'Twas in the moon of win-ter time When all the birds had fled, That Migh-ty Git-chi-Man-i-tou Sent an-gel-choirs in-stead; Be-fore their light the stars grew dim, And wond-'ring hun-ters heard the hymn—Je-sus your King is born, Je-sus is born, In ex-cel-sis glo-ri-a.

The Huron Carol

2.

Within a lodge of broken bark the tender babe was found,
A ragged robe of rabbit skin enwrapp'd his beauty 'round;
But as the hunter braves drew nigh,
The Angel-song rang loud and high—
Jesus your King is born,
Jesus is born,
In excelsis gloria.

3.

The earliest moon of winter time is not so round and fair
As was the ring of glory on the helpless infant there.
The Chiefs from far before him knelt,
With gifts of fox and beaver pelt.
Jesus your King is born,
Jesus is born,
In excelsis gloria.

4.

O children of the forest free, O sons of Manitou,
The Holy Child of earth and heaven is born today for you.
Come kneel before the radiant Boy,
Who brings you beauty, peace, and joy.
Jesus your King is born,
Jesus is born,
In excelsis gloria.

Note: Gitchi-Manitou means 'Great Spirit'—or 'God'
This Carol is reproduced by permission of copyright owner:
The Frederick Harris Music Co. Limited, Oakville, Ontario.

Republic of China

A Brownie in the Republic of China wears a green cap and a green dress with a green belt and a yellow tie. Her Brownie pin is a frog on the national flower, and its colour shows her progress with her Brownie tests. She is given a silver pin when she passes her first tests; then it is changed to a golden pin and finally to a green pin as she becomes older and succeeds with harder tests. Like all Brownies, her Promise, Law and Motto remind her to help other people as much as she can.

Testwork for Brownies in China

The Brownies of China have tests very much like ours. They learn about their flag as one of their Golden Bar tests, and they also learn to tell the time, and to use correctly the dishes, spoons and chopsticks on the table at meal times.

For three of the Golden Hand tests, a Brownie learns how to plant and grow, as well as to cut and arrange flowers. She must wash or peel fruit and prepare a fruit salad, and she learns how to clean and polish brass or silver.

Good Turns

Brownies in China do many Good Turns around their homes, and they are very helpful with younger brothers and sisters. They love to act little plays to entertain other people, and they cut out and make some of their "dressing up" clothes, such as collars, capes, and cuffs of material or paper.

Two Games Chinese Brownies Like To Play

"Lame Chicken"

Each of the teams (Sixes) has ten sticks (or slippers or anything else suitable). These are placed 10-12 inches apart like rungs of a ladder—one row in front of each team and several feet away from the players. The first Brownie in each Six is the "lame chicken"; she must hop over these sticks without touching them. After hopping over the last stick, she reaches down, and picks up the stick and hops back with it and places it at the beginning. The next Brownie then becomes the "lame chicken".

A Brownie is disqualified if she touches both feet to the ground or touches a stick with her feet, when hopping.

"Water Sprite"

Two lines of Brownies face one another, 20 to 60 feet apart. Between the two lines, stands the Water Sprite; the space between is a river.

The Water Sprite beckons to one of the Brownies to leave the bank and cross the river. Immediately she covers her eyes and counts to ten. The Brownie to whom she signalled, now signals to a Brownie on the opposite bank while the Water Sprite has her eyes covered. These two Brownies then try to change places while the Water Sprite tries to catch one of them. When she succeeds, the Brownie caught, becomes the next Water Sprite.

Language

Many Brownies in China speak Mandarin. Here are three greetings they use.

Good morning 早安! tsao an (jow arn)

Thank you 謝!謝! hsieh hsieh (zay zay)

Goodbye 再見! tsai chien (Chai jen)

Things to do

Ask Brown Owl if she has a copy of Brownie Stories of the World—Book 5. Then read in it the Brownie Story for China and find out why the Brownie pin has a frog on it.

Could you find out what the flag of The Republic of China looks like, and then make a model flag-pole with this Chinese flag?

Have you ever eaten a Chinese meal?

16

Colombia

Colombia is a hot country in South America which grows coffee, bananas, sugar and rice. There are many gaily coloured birds including blue and yellow macaws.

The Brownies in Colombia wear blue-grey skirts with shoulder straps, and white blouses with yellow scarves round their necks.

Activities for Brownies in Colombia

The Brownies and their leaders share their ideas and plan their meetings so they can have fun learning new things to do for themselves and other people. They are proud of their country and try hard to be kind and helpful people in today's world.

Good Turns

The Brownies in Colombia help their parents with household jobs; they help to keep their schools tidy; they look after and play with smaller children, especially in recreation programmes set up for under-privileged children.

A Game Colombian Brownies Like to Play

"Juan Palmada"   (wan pal-may-da)

(Johnny Clap-Hands)

The Brownies make a circle, leaving one space in it. Two Brownies stand back to back, outside the circle, by the space. At a signal, these two run in opposite directions round the circle. When they meet, each jumps into the air and claps hands (overhead) with the other. Then they continue running to see which one can reach the empty space first. The loser chooses another girl to take her place and the game continues. Anyone who loses three times, must "pay a forfeit" chosen by the Pack.

(Forfeits may be of wide variety; recite a verse, turn a somersault, find three round pebbles, etc.)

A Craft Enjoyed by Brownies in Colombia

Canadian Brownies now have a Puppetry badge and so do Colombian Brownies. They make their own puppets and invent their own plays. Then they invite their parents to a performance which is given to raise money for the Pack or to help other people.

This is how the Brownies make heads for their puppets. The end of a sock is filled with rice, and a stick about 1½ inches in diameter and several inches long, is pushed in. The sock is tied tightly and this gives a round shape to work with. Some glue is made of flour with a little water, cooked in a saucepan. This is used to stick on strips of newspaper several layers thick; the Brownie holds the stick while doing this. Eyebrows, nose, etc. are made from pulpy wet newspaper squeezed with some of the glue. Then the head is dried outside or in a not-too-hot oven.

When dry, the stick is removed, the rice poured out, and with great care, the sock is pulled out. The head is painted, a neck shaped in the hole, a wig may be added, and the puppet dressed in a glove-like garment. The Brownie works her puppet with her index finger in the neck, and her thumb and either ring or little finger for the arms and hands.

Language

Colombian Brownies speak Spanish. Here are three greetings they use.

Good day	Buenos Dias	(bwen-ose-dee-as)
Thank you	Gracias	(grat-zee-as)
Goodbye	Adios	(add-e-ose)

Things to do

See if you can make a puppet the way Colombian Brownies do.

A great deal of coffee comes from Colombia. Could you find out how it is grown and sent to Canada?

Denmark

Denmark is a beautiful country with lakes and woods and many farms and ocean beaches, but it has no mountains.

There are three different Brownie groups in Denmark. A Brownie in the Y.W.C.A. Girl Guides wears a green uniform and she is called a Grønsmutte, which is a wren. In a Grønsmutte Pack there are only girls. A Brownie in the Danish Baptist Association wears a blue uniform and she is called a lark, a cheerful little bird often seen in the country-side in Denmark. A Brownie in the blue uniform of the Danish Scout and Guide Association is called a Blämejse (blow-my-se) which means Bluetit, a little bird rather like our chickadee. In a Blämejse Pack, there are Cub Scouts too.

Activities for Brownies in Denmark.

Danish Brownies do not have testwork, but there are many Interest badges. Sometimes the Brownies do things just for fun; sometimes to earn a badge. They are interested in a great many different things, such as camping, handicrafts, their own country, and training their senses to enjoy and care for the world around them.

All Brownies learn how to behave outdoors without hurting plants or animals. They are careful to observe these "Nevers".

Never use an axe or knife on a living tree.

Never break branches from living trees or bushes.

Never walk through a plantation of young trees.

Never gather too many flowers from one spot; be careful to leave the roots.

Never walk across cultivated soil.

Never walk or climb on stone walls.

Never leave litter in the out of doors; better to remove litter left by others.

Never touch young wild animals or remove birds' eggs.

Never hurt birds' nests or other animals' homes.

Brownies always remember to be obedient to gamekeepers and other people looking after nature.

They always try to be quiet . . . animals living in woods and fields will be scared by noise.

Brownies in Denmark have interest badges as Canadian Brownies do. One of them is called "Children in other countries". The Brownie will do some or all of these:—

Sing a song about children in other countries.

Join in a game from another country.

Sing a children's song from another country.

Draw or find pictures to show how different are children's homes in another country.

Draw a foreign child in national costume.

Know a folk tale from another country and make a drawing for it.

Sometimes the Pack works in small groups so the Brownies can tell each other about the different countries they have chosen.

Good Turns

Brownies try to be helpful all the year round, but each September, all Brownies, Guides and Scouts in Denmark join in a special good turn called Spejderhjaelpen (spy-der-yel-pen). During one week, they do all kinds of different jobs; baby-sitting, car-cleaning, housework, gardening, shopping, etc.; during this week, they are paid for the jobs. In ten years they have earned more than five million Danish Kroner (about $700,000). This money is used to help children and provide medical treatment in countries where it is needed. A great deal has gone to a leprosy centre in India and another part has gone to help the Eskimo children in Greenland. The motto for Spejderhjaelpen is "Sound children help sick children".

A Game Danish Brownies Like to Play

"Good Morning, Good Afternoon, Good Evening"

The Brownies make a circle, One Brownie runs round the outside of the circle and gives one of the others a pat on the back as she passes. This Brownie then runs the other way round the circle and when the two meet, they each give the Brownie salute, and say "Good Morning". They go on running till they meet again, say "Good Afternoon", run on once more, meet and shake hands, saying "Good Evening", and then run on to reach the empty place in the circle.

Language

Brownies in Denmark speak Danish and they learn English in school. Here are a few Danish words:

Good day	God Dag	(Go-day)
Goodbye	Farvel	(Far-vel)
Thank you	Tak	(Tak)

Something to do

Danish Brownies enjoy making things like all Brownies do. This is how they sometimes make an autograph book or notebook.

First, some gay coloured leaves are chosen and carefully pressed for a few days between newspapers under a heavy weight. Then each leaf is put on a piece of paper and a little sheet of clear contact plastic, gummed side down, is placed on top. Several pieces of paper the same size are folded with this cover and stapled together to make a pocket sized book. Sometimes the paper is carefully cut round the edges of the leaf to make a leaf-shaped book.

Now perhaps you could try to make yourself "a maple leaf book" or make a "leaf picture" working this way with a larger piece of coloured cardboard and gummed plastic.

At Christmas time, Brownies in Denmark make Christmas hearts. They fill them with candy or tiny gifts and hang them on the Christmas tree. Could you make some too?

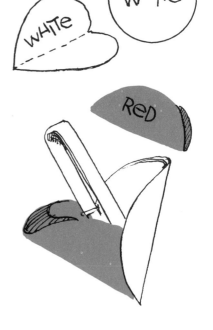

Cut out two circles, one of red paper and one of white (draw round a large cup first). Fold each circle in half; glue them together, and put on a paper handle.

See if you can make some Danish "open sandwiches". Each has three main parts:—one slice of buttered bread, completely covered by a topping of cheese, cooked chicken, ham, salami, bacon, shrimps, fish, hard boiled eggs, etc., and a colourful garnish of a slice of tomato, cucumber, lemon, radish, watercress, green or red pepper, cream cheese, or salad dressing, etc.

Look in a supermarket and see if you can find any foods that come from Denmark. The Danes are famous too, for the beautiful furniture and china they make.

Hans Christian Andersen, writer of the famous fairy tales, lived in Denmark. The page at the beginning of this section shows a drawing of the Little Mermaid from one of his stories. Could you borrow Andersen's Fairy Tales from your library? There are several stories you might enjoy.

Here is Andersen's story of The Princess and the Pea. It is a lovely story to mime while two Brownies take it in turn to read the story. Ask Brown Owl if you may do this at a Pack meeting.

"The Princess and the Pea"
by Hans Christian Andersen

Once upon a time, there was a Prince who wanted to find a real princess to be his wife . . . so he travelled all over the world to find one . . . There were princesses in plenty, but there was always something not perfectly correct, so he returned home very much cast down, for he did so want a real princess for his bride.

One evening, there was a terrible storm, and while the rain was pouring down, there came a knock at the palace door . . . and the old King himself went to open it . . . A princess was standing outside begging for shelter, and she said she was a REAL princess . . .

The Queen was determined to find out if this were true, so she went into the bedroom . . . Then she put 20 mattresses and 20 eiderdowns on top of the pea . . . There, the princess slept for the night.

In the morning, they asked her how she had slept . . . and she said that she had hardly closed her eyes all night, for there had been something in the bed which had made her black and blue all over . . . Then they could see this was a real princess, for nobody else could possibly have such a tender skin . . .

So the Prince married her . . . and the pea was carried in the wedding procession . . . Afterwards, the pea was carefully kept in the Museum, where it is still to be seen to this day, unless someone has taken it away.

A Fishing Game

This is a game Danish Brownies play.

The fishing poles are made from thin wooden dowel rods about nine inches long. A small screw eye is put into one end of each pole; then a heavy thread about seven inches long is tied into the screw eye, and on the other end, a dress hook is tied. This completes the fishing poles, though they may be painted different colours if desired.

The fish are made from corks about one inch high. Staples or tiny hasps are driven into the tops of the fish, and the fish are each given numbers between one and twenty, written on the bottoms. The fish should be painted. They are placed on the table or the floor, not floated in water.

Four players fish at once, by catching the dress hook on the end of the fishing line into the staple on the fish. As soon as one fish is caught, he is unhooked and another is gone after. At the close of the game, the player who has caught the most pounds of fish (from the numbers counted on the bottoms) wins the game. The number of fish caught does not count.

Germany

Many of the world's great musicians and story-tellers and wood-carvers have come from Germany, and it was here some of our favourite carols were written.

There are three different Brownie groups in Germany. The VCP is for Protestant girls, the PSG is for Catholic girls and the BdP is an association for both boys and girls. The VCP and the PSG Brownies do not have a special Brownie uniform; they both wear Guide uniform and for ordinary meetings they wear T-shirts, the VCP having blue ones with white trefoils on them and the PSG having light blue ones with dark blue trefoils. The Brownies in these two groups are called Wichtel (vick-tell). The Brownies and Cubs of the BdP groups are called Wölflinge, and they wear dark blue blouses with yellow scarves. Their enrolment pins of wolf heads are worn on the left pockets of their uniforms.

Activities for Brownies in Germany

German Brownies have activities very much like ours in Canada. They like to make things and to go exploring in the outdoors. They can earn Interest badges and go to camp.

A Game German Brownies Like to Play

"Frogs in the Pond"

Draw and cut out little frogs from tissue paper, one for each team. Make a circle with chalk or rope about 12 feet ahead of each starting line. Each team has an old newspaper folded into quarter size. The frogs are put on the floor at the starting line and the first Brownies in each team "fan" with their newspapers to make the frogs move to their ponds. When this is done, each Brownie takes her frog out of the pond and runs back to the second Brownie. Now it is her turn to move the frog into the pond.

When everyone in the team has put the frog into its pond, that team sits down. The first team sitting down is the winner.

Language

Brownies in Germany speak German. Here are a few German words.

Good day	Guten Tag	(goo-ten-tag)
Thank you	Danke	(dan-ker)
Goodbye	Auf Wiedersehen	(owf-ve-der-sain)

Something to do

Brownies in Germany like to make things. Here are two favourites. Perhaps you could make them too.

A Wall Picture

On a piece of cardboard (black or coloured, if possible) the Brownie draws a shape or picture. She puts some glue on these shapes, and on top of the glue, she puts little cut-out pieces of material or lengths of coloured wool. This makes a gay picture for the wall of her room or to give away as a gift.

Paper Bag Masks

For Carnival Days, Brownies in Germany make masks out of large paper bags. They cut out holes for the eyes and mouth, and make hair with wool or paper strips, glued or stapled on. Then they colour the rest of the face with paints or crayons.

The custom of decorating and lighting Christmas trees came from Germany too. See what you can find out about this. Perhaps you could make a tiny Christmas tree and decorate it for someone who is ill at Christmas.

The Oberammergau Passion Play is acted every tenth year in the Black Forest part of Germany. It has an interesting story behind it. Could you find out about it?

Greece

Brownies in Greece are called Poulia (poo-lee-ah) which means Birds. They wear dark brown jumpers with yellow shirts and scarves printed with yellow, dark and light brown stripes and trefoils on them. The Promise pins of little gold birds are worn on the scarves. The caps are green with yellow stripes and the Greek Brownies wear their badges on their caps.

Greece is a country of mountains and sea-coast, sunshine and beautiful climate. Delicious fruits grow there and bees make honey from the wild flowers. The history of Greece begins many centuries before the birth of Christ. Some of the world's most famous men in art and literature and science were born in Greece.

Activities for Brownies in Greece

Here are a few of the activities a Greek Brownie does: Think what would make a member of her family happy and do it in her leisure time.

Learn the Greek games which children have been playing for thousands of years.

Learn about the traditional food, customs and celebrations of her own town or village.

Watch a craftsman and describe his work.

Good Turns

Greek Brownies help at home in many ways as all Brownies do. Recently, (among other good turns) they started drawing old houses, gates, windows, etc., trying to keep alive the architecture of old times, in case it disappears in modern building developments.

NORTHERN
GREECE

SOUTHERN
GREECE

Designs of old Greek houses made by Brownies of Greece.
The architecture is typical of each region of the country.

A Game Greek Brownies Like to Play

"The Puppet"

This is a very old game which has been played by children in Greece for thousands of years.

One Brownie is chosen to be the Mother and she stands outside a circle of Brownies, all sitting cross-legged. A "puppet doll" has been made out of a handkerchief or piece of material, or a scarf, and this is passed quickly round the circle from Brownie to the next Brownie in either direction so that the "Mother" cannot catch it, as she runs round the outside of the circle. When she does at last, get "her child", she changes places with the Brownie who was holding it at the time.

Language

The alphabet of the Greek language is written in a different way from ours, but here are a few words in Greek in our kind of printing.

Good day	Kalimèra	(kally-mèra)
Thank you	Efcharistò	(ef-cha-ri-stò)
Goodbye	Yàssou	(yà-ssou)

Things to do

Pottery is a very old Greek craft. Perhaps you could get a ball of clay and see if you can work like the Greek Brownies do. This is how you can make a little bowl:

Roll the ball of clay in the palms of your dampened hands; then press both thumbs into the middle of it. Keep pressing with one thumb while your other hand turns the clay. Go on doing this, dampening your hands when needed, till the bowl is an even thickness all round.

Put the bowl on the table, and flatten the bottom of it by pressing gently with your thumbs from the inside. Smooth the inside and the outside once again with your dampened fingers.

You may be lucky enough to know someone who will fire (bake) your clay bowl for you in a special oven called a kiln.

Ireland

Brownies in Ireland wear royal blue uniform dresses and wool caps of the same colour. The different badges are placed almost exactly the same as ours.

Ireland is a beautiful island, with grass and trees so green, that it is sometimes called The Emerald Isle. It was here that St. Patrick went, many years ago, to tell the people about God. It is said that he found the land so full of snakes that his first act was to make a drum and taking two sticks to beat it, he went through the land beating his drum till his arms grew helpless with weariness. The snakes wriggled into a large tin box, which was fastened tightly and thrown into the sea. Some people say that the movement of the waves is caused by the snakes trying to get out of the box.

There is a special day for St. Patrick on March 17th, and shamrocks are worn to remember how he picked them to explain to the people of Ireland that "God is three Persons in One".

Testwork for Brownies in Ireland

Brownies in Ireland have Golden Bar, Golden Ladder and Golden Hand badges just the same as we do in Canada. Some of the tests are a little different from ours. A Brownie must be able to tell the time; and describe and draw the National flag. For part of her Golden Hand badge, she must make a little book on Safety in the Home. She must put in it some drawings or cut-out pictures and write something about six rules for safety in her home.

Good Turns

Irish Brownies do good turns at home every day just like you do but sometimes, the whole Pack does a good turn together. They visit old people, read to them, take their dogs for walks, help them with their gardens and sing carols to them at Christmas time. One pack went into the country one day and picked blackberries which they made into jam for old people.

In December, many Brownies make and fill Christmas stockings. Then on a certain day, at a certain time, the Brownies (and Guides and Rangers too) take their stockings to a pick-up point, where a driver arrives in a car, or wagon or truck, to collect the stockings ready to take them to needy families for Christmas.

Packs take part in clearing litter from the seashore, public parks, church grounds and so on. One Pack even made a wayside garden on some unused land in their village.

Some Brownies have helped too, at sponsored Knit Weekends. The six-inch squares they knitted were made into blankets and the sponsor money went with the blankets to an Old People's Housing project.

Two Games Irish Brownies Like to Play

"Going Down O'Connell Street"
(the main street in Dublin, the capital city of Ireland)

Brown Owl says, "As I was going down O'Connell Street, I saw a man cleaning a shop window.".

All the Brownies act this, and Brown Owl chooses one who is acting well, to direct the game for the next turn.

The Brownie says, "As I was going down O'Connell Street, I saw a boy riding a bicycle.".

The Brownies act this and the Brownie who called, chooses the next Brownie so the game can continue.

"Tangle Tree Woods"

Divide the pack into two sides; one side are the Old Men of the Woods and the other side are the Old Women. They stand at opposite ends of the room or playground. The Old Men come over to the Old Women, hobbling and stiff, saying, "We're the old men of Tangle Tree Woods".

The Old Women say, "What can you do?"

The Old Men answer, "We can do anything."

The Old Women say, "Work away then."

The Old Men then act something they have already decided upon such as washing, sawing wood, etc., and the Old Women call out when they have guessed what the Old Men are doing. If it is correct, the Old Men run away and the Old Women chase them. Any Old Man who is caught, becomes an Old Woman.

Then the game is repeated with the Old Women coming over to the Old Men.

40

Language

Irish Brownies speak English, but many of them
also speak the Gaelic which they learn in school.
Here are a few words in Gaelic.

Good day	Dia dhuit	(dee-ag-wich)
Thank you	Go raibh maith agat	(gura-moh-a-guth)
Goodbye	Slán	(slawn)

Things to do

Here is something that an Irish Brownie enjoys making; a mat for Pow-
wow.

Fold twelve separate sheets of
newspaper into strips about two
inches wide. Lay six of them
beside each other on the table
and weave the other six into
them. Tuck in the alternate
ends. These mats can be
painted and varnished and will
last a long time.

Perhaps your Pack could make some to use for Pow-wow or on a
Brownie Holiday.

Go to the library and ask if you may borrow a book of Irish Folk-tales. See if you can find out about Leprechauns, the special Irish fairies.

Perhaps your parents, or teacher, or Brown Owl will help you to learn to sing an Irish song or to dance an Irish jig.

You might make an Irish scrapbook and write in it, a story of your own about Leprechauns or Shamrocks.

Did you know that potatoes are a favourite food in Ireland? Could you make some potato scones for your family?

To make 12 scones, you will need:

1½ cups of cold mashed potatoes   1 egg beaten

1 cup prepared biscuit flour   A dash of pepper and salt

(also, if you wish, a tablespoon of grated onion)

Mix all these together, adding milk if too stiff.
Roll out about ½ inch thick (like pastry, on a floured board)
Cut out scones with a 3-inch round cutter
Fry in butter or bacon fat till brown
Delicious alone or with bacon or any other meat.

Nigeria

Nigeria is a large country in Africa where it is very hot. There are two well-marked seasons; the rains last from April to October and the dry season is from November until March.

The Brownie wears a brown dress with short sleeves and a yellow tie.

Testwork for Brownies in Nigeria

Brownies in Nigeria have many tests the same as Canadian Brownies. A different one is sewing. A Brownie must make something useful with a turned down hem, putting some stitches on to decorate it. Before she goes to Guides, she must learn three of the knots she will need to use, perhaps at camp. Some tests have to be adapted for certain parts of this large country.

Good Turns

Brownie Packs help to plant flowers and bushes in public parks and on "islands" at road crossings, so that they will give shade and be beautiful to look at.

Most Nigerian towns and villages have a market, which is usually an open outdoor place. Brownies sweep it to help to keep it clean and neat. They also scrub and clean slippery steps in public places, so that old people and little children will not fall and hurt themselves.

Brownies sometimes go with their leaders to help to clear up and burn outdoor refuse for old or handicapped people.

A Game Nigerian (Yoruba speaking) Brownies Play

There is a special game played during the cassava season in Nigeria's western state. Cassava is a plant which is peeled, soaked and strained and made into flour called elubo (a-loo-bo). Every day, the farmer's family stand around a lawn, or mats or big wooden trays, with yam sacks by their sides. With clean hands or bowls, they spread out the cassava to dry, repeating this rhyme.

Ìsánsálùbó

Ìsánsālùbó (ee-săn-să-loo-bŏ)   Chorus Perepe (pĕ-rĕ-pĕ)
Òní mō sálùbó (ō-nee mŏ să-loo-bŏ)   Chorus Perepe (pĕ-rĕ-pĕ)
Òlā mō sálùbó (ŏ-lah mŏ să-loo-bŏ)   Chorus Perepe (pĕ-rĕ-pĕ)
Èlùbó mí kò gbē (ā-loo-bŏ mē kō gbee)   Chorus Perepe (pĕ-rĕ-pĕ)
Õkān mì nù (ō-kown mē noo)   Chorus Mayawa (mă-yă-wă)

Down   Up   - Middle or Flat   ˜ Slur or Drag

In the evening, the people pack the flour back into the bags. This they do daily until the cassava is perfectly dry. Then it is pounded and sifted ready for use.

This is the game the Brownies play in the cassava season. They all stand in a large circle with one Brownie in the middle. She says the rhyme, line by line, while the others echo the chorus in rhythm. As they chant, they bend and move forward very slowly till they meet in the centre. At the same time, they stretch their hands forwards and backwards pretending to spread the partly-made flour on the lawn. At the last line, the Brownie in the middle is exclaiming she has dropped her money. All wave their hands left and right as they say the last chorus, moving backwards to their places in the circle.

Language

There are several different languages spoken in Nigeria. Here are three greetings in the Yoruba language.

Good morning	Eku Aro	(ĕ karŏ)
Thank you	A dupẹ	(ah doo-pĕ)
Goodbye	O dìgbà o	(oh deeg-bah oh)

Things to do

Brownies in Nigeria enjoy making all kinds of things using raffia, such as belts, bags, table mats, fans, etc.

Perhaps you could try to make a raffia mat. Braid several long strands of raffia, adding more raffia just before you finish each set of strands. Then bend your braided strip and stitch it together so that it makes a flat round or square mat. You can also make a simple bowl this way, but you will need to braid thicker strips to coil.

Nigeria grows cocoa trees which help to make our chocolate candy bars. Try to find out how the cocoa beans become chocolate.

Philippines

The Philippines is a group of islands in the Pacific Ocean. It is usually very hot there, and the Brownies may never have seen snow or ice.

A Brownie of the Philippines is called a Star Scout. She wears a green dress printed with trefoil designs with a belt and cap of the same material. As she earns her interest badges they are sewn on a badge scarf which she wears across her right shoulder.

A troop of Filipino Star Scouts is divided into Clusters (Sixes). The leader of a cluster is called a Bright Star and the Troop Leader is called the North Star.

Testwork for Brownies in the Philippines

One test says: "Find out with your Cluster, how you may be of service to your church and in your home. Ask your parents to help you find this out."

Here is another test which a Filipino Brownie enjoys doing. She learns about a Filipino legend, and with some other Stars (Brownies) tells it to the troop by acting or miming the story.

Good Turns

Filipino Brownies gather flowers and take them to patients in hospitals. They bring Father's slippers to him as soon as he gets home from work each day. They help Mother by dusting furniture, taking care of small brothers and sisters, and going on errands and relaying messages.

A Game Filipino Brownies Like to Play

"Presohan"
(for 5 or more players)

Every Brownie has an empty can. One Brownie (the prisoner) puts her can on the ground about 5 large paces from the other Brownies who stand on a straight line, cans in hand, facing her.

One Brownie starts the game by throwing her can at the prisoner's can, to knock it out of place. If she does this, and is able to get her own can back again without being caught by the prisoner, she may do so. Otherwise she waits until another Brownie hits the prisoner's can, whereupon she may run and recover her own can. The prisoner, after putting her own can back in place, may "tag" (catch) any of the Brownies who tries to get back her cans. Any Brownie "tagged", becomes the next prisoner.

Language

The national language of the Philippines is called Pilipino but many people speak English and Spanish; here are a few words in Pilipino that Brownies use.

Good morning	Magandang Umaga	(mah-gan-dang u-mah-gah)
Thank you	Maraming Salamat	(mah-rah-ming sah-lah-mat)
Goodbye	Paalam	(pah-ah-lam)

Something to do

The Brownies in the Philippines enjoy making necklaces, bracelets and rings out of the seeds from fruit. This is how it is done.

If the seeds are hard, they are boiled till soft and then dried in the sun. The Brownie then cuts a thread long enough for whatever she needs to make and threads her needle. She sews the seeds together, often making a pattern with different kinds of seeds.

Perhaps you can find some melon or other seeds and try doing this.

Bananas and coconuts grow in the Philippines, and the Brownies use the leaves of these trees to make toys and useful articles like mats and baskets.

Could you try to braid a grass mat, or make a little basket using leaves from bulrushes, or other plants?

United Kingdom

(England, Wales, Scotland and Ulster)

Brownies in the United Kingdom are all between seven and ten years old. They wear a brown uniform with two pockets, brown hats and yellow ties crossed in front.

They try to keep the Brownie Promise while they are busy helping at home, making things, lending a hand, keeping fit, being wide-awake, being friendly, having fun out of doors and doing their best all the time.

Pack meetings are great fun as the Brownies take part in Ventures, Journeys, Interest Badges and all kinds of games, ceremonies, acting, stories and secrets.

Pack Ventures are Brownie adventures planned by the Pack in Pow-wow, and everyone has a part. Some Brownies have made gifts for other people, raised money, given parties and concerts, held sports days and many other things.

One of the best possible Ventures is to go on Pack Holiday. The Pack borrows a house, school or Church Hall and turns it into the Pack home for several days. The Brownies have great fun cooking, cleaning and looking after the house, as well as exploring, having picnics and expeditions, making things, playing games and listening to stories.

Brownies can also take part in Journeys, of which there are three — the Footpath, the Road, the Highway. Each Journey is made up of interesting challenges, from which the Brownie chooses something that she has not done before, or does it in a new or more difficult way. Here are some of the things that a Brownie may choose to do: painting or making models; doing cleaning or tidying jobs; doing something better than before with a ball or hoop; making equipment for the Pack; growing a plant from seed or bulb; helping to make a Pack Prayer Book or "Thank You, God" chart; finding out about Brownies in other countries.

A Brownie can meet several Journey challenges while taking part in Ventures or while working for an Interest badge. There are about thirty Interest badges for which Brownies can work if they have particular interests or hobbies.

Good Turns

When Brownies have learned to do something and have practised it, they try very hard to find a new way of doing it as a good turn or a Venture. The handbook for Brownies in the United Kingdom says this about the motto, "Lend a Hand".

"Have you ever tried to feed a baby, take a pan off the stove, let the cat out, answer the telephone and pop an apple tart in the oven all at the same time?
Maybe not . . . but ever so many mothers have tried to. And they just haven't enough hands.

Have you ever tried to write on a blackboard, work out a difficult sum, stop a paint pot from upsetting, catch a newt[1] before it escapes and pull someone's splinter[2] all at the same time?

Maybe not, but ever so many teachers have tried to. And they just haven't enough hands.

Have you ever tried to carry two shopping baskets and a handbag[3], find the right change, pick up a penny you have dropped, keep your dog out of a fight and give an ice-cream to your small boy?

Maybe not, but ever so many shoppers have tried to. And they just haven't enough hands."

In fact, thousands of people every day need the help of an extra hand, so that is why the Brownie Motto is LEND A HAND. Brownies keep their eyes open and try to lend a hand whenever they see they are needed."

1. water lizard like a salamander. 2. sliver. 3. purse.

Two Games Brownies in the United Kingdom Like to Play

"The Witch's Glue Pots"

Brown Owl is a Glue Witch and is sticky all over! Any Brownie caught by her, sticks to her until she is placed in one of the witch's four glue pots. (These are circles about two yards in diameter, drawn in chalk or marked out with cord in various parts of the room or playground.) Anyone in a glue pot becomes sticky, and by leaning out of the pot, but keeping her feet firmly in it, can catch any Brownie running past her. The last one to be caught can be the witch next time.

"Rainbow Tag"

For this game, a box of counters of 3 or 4 different colours is needed. Every Brownie, except two who are chasers, has a counter which she holds so that the colour cannot be seen. At "Go!" the chasers run after the Pack. Anyone caught must give up her counter; she may then go to Brown Owl for another one, and continue in the game. The first chaser to have in her hand 3 counters of 3 different colours shouts "Stop!" and is the winner of that turn.

Two Handcraft Activities that British Brownies Enjoy

"Scribble Prints"

Lay a leaf, vein side up on a hard table. Place a piece of thin paper over the leaf. Rub across the paper with the side of a wax crayon and the outline of the leaf and its veins will appear as you rub.

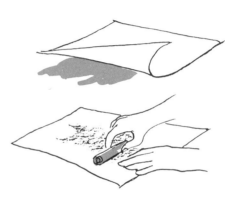

These prints can be cut out to make leaf collections or put together to make leaf people or animals.

"Spatter Prints"

A leaf or any flat cardboard cut-out shape is fixed firmly with pins on a piece of white paper. The Brownie dips an old toothbrush in some paint, and holding it near the edge of the paper, draws a piece of wood or card gently towards her over the bristles. This makes a light spray fall on the piece of paper so that when the leaf or shape is taken away, its pattern is clearly seen in the middle of the spatter.

Things to do

England has a special saint called St. George. Perhaps you could find the story of how he killed a dragon, and get your Six to help you act it for the Pack.

See if you can find a picture of the flag of the United Kingdom. It is called the Union flag.

You could make a scrapbook of the Queen and her family or a scrapbook of London with pictures of some of the famous buildings.

You could collect some postage stamps from the United Kingdom.

Walk around the stores and find out if there are any packets of cookies or candies which have come from the United Kingdom.

Ulster grows a great deal of the world's flax, which is made into linen. Look at the edges of coloured tea towels and you may see the words, Made in Northern Ireland or Made in Ulster.

Some of you may learn Scottish dancing; can you find out the names of some of the tartans worn in Scotland?

Prince Charles is Prince of Wales. Wales has many famous castles. Could you borrow a library book and find a picture of a Welsh castle. Perhaps you could draw or paint a picture of it.

The Brownies of the United Kingdom have a special magazine of their own called The Brownie. It is published each week and is full of stories and news about Brownie events. Brownies in many Commonwealth countries write to England to order a subscription to this magazine, and they also write to the Editor telling some of their news. If you have saved up some money, or if someone offers to give you this gift, write to:

>Subscription Department, (The Brownie)
>Girl Guides Association,
>17-19 Buckingham Palace Road,
>London, SW1W OPT
>England.

The subscription will cost about $18.00 for a year. This is quite a lot of money; perhaps Brown Owl would order a copy to be shared by the Pack.

United States

Brownie Girl Scouts in the United States are six, seven and eight years old. They join together in troops and do activities around the Brownie B's. (Be a Discoverer, Be a Ready-Helper and Be a Friend-maker). Brownie troops are full of Brownie Magic with plans being made in a Brownie Ring and dues money being called Brownie Gold.

The Brownies have a variety of uniforms: a brown jumper, or shorts, or long pants, worn with a tangerine knit top or a white blouse with brown trefoil stripes, and a tangerine tie. The little brown cap is called a beanie.

Brownies may work on the Brownie B patches. These are activities designed to allow girls to learn more about the Brownie B's. For each year in the patch plan, the Brownie receives a pie-shaped patch which can be worn on her uniform. Brownies may also learn more about Junior Girl Scouts and receive a Bridge to Juniors patch.

A Brownie often goes on hikes to discover the world out-doors, and in the summer, she may go to Day Camp with other troops. She discovers the fun of painting and modelling, and of making music by singing and using instruments she may have helped to make. She discovers the Land of Let's Pretend, with its stories and acting and dancing. Home, too, is a good place to find out things, especially with her family there to help her.

One of the Brownie's biggest discoveries is finding out she can be a Ready Helper. First, she does things for herself, and then she does Lend a Hand jobs round her home. While doing these things, she also is being a Friend-Maker among her family, her school-mates, her Brownie troop and round her neighbourhood.

Because she is a Brownie, she has Brownie friends too, all round the world. At some of her troop meetings, she will find out more about these Kabouters in the Netherlands, the Fadas in Brazil, the Meiser in Norway and many others.

Good Turns

A Brownie in the United States sometimes "gives herself" as a gift to Mother, especially on Mother's Day. She makes a gift coupon for each job she promises to do. Then she puts all the coupons together in a little book, and makes a gay cover for it. Perhaps you could do this too, sometime, as a surprise for mother.

Brownie Scouts are very enthusiastic about caring for their environment. There is a special book for them called Eco-Antics. In it are suggestions for fascinating activities such as:- "Make Your Own Re-cycled Paper," "How Polluted is the Air? Find Out!" "Catch a Snowflake." You can order this book price $1.25 from Girl Scouts of U.S.A., 830 Third Avenue, New York City, N.Y. 10022.

Here is a small copy of one of its pages.

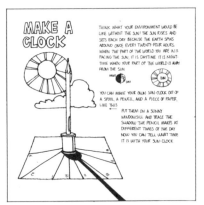

From "Eco-Antics", copyright 1974. Girl Scouts of the U.S.A. Used by permission.

Two Games American Brownies Like to Play

"Barnyard Bedlam"

Brown Owl hides plenty of pine cones, beans, macaroni pieces or other small objects within a certain area, preferably outside.

The Brownies are divided into Sixes with the Sixer in charge of each Six. Each team chooses an animal name. The Six then search for the hidden objects, but the Sixer is the only one who may pick them up. If a member of a Six finds an object, she makes the noise of the animal her Six represents. This calls the Sixer who comes to pick up all the objects which her team finds. The Six with the largest number wins.

Frog in the Sea.

This game can be played in a large room or on a playground or in shallow water.

Five Brownies are chosen to be "frogs" and they sit cross-legged in a circle, facing outwards. The other Brownies make a circle round the "frogs" and skip (if on land) or walk (if in the water) repeating: "Frog in the sea, can't catch me!" The "frogs" try to tag any Brownie, without rising or uncrossing their legs. When a Brownie is caught, she changes places with the "frog" who caught her.

Things to do

Brownies in the United States are clever at making "nature toys" like the pioneers did. Could you make a corn husk doll like they do?

Use dried corn husks. Dip them in water to make them soft and easy to work with.

Fold a large husk in half. Stuff the top half with a wad of husks to make a head.

Wind thread or string tightly round to make a neck.

For arms, fold another husk. Make hands by winding thread at both ends. Tie tightly.

Slip arms through body. Tie body to keep arms in place.

For a wide skirt, tie more husks on at the waist. Cut the bottom of the skirt straight so the doll will stand.

Draw or paste on a face and hair. What could you use for a hat?

Could you find out how the Pilgrims held the first Thanksgiving in the New England states?

Brownies in New York City can see the United Nations Building. Do you know what goes on there? You may already know about U.N.I.C.E.F. If not, you could find out from your teacher or Brown Owl.

What does the flag of the United States look like? Could you draw and colour it correctly?

Do you have a stamp collection? There are many, many stamps of the United States.

Canada has a beaver emblem. Do you know what the United States has? Could you find out something more about it?

The Brownie Girl Scouts have a special "magazine" called DAISY. In it are all kinds of Brownie things to read and do. Sometimes, there is a page for the Brownies' own letters and drawings. If you are very lucky, your parents or some other kind person might give you a year's subscription for a birthday or Christmas gift. Send $3.80 to: ($7.00 for 2 years).

DAISY,
830 Third Ave.,
New York City,
N.Y. 10022
U.S.A.

Do You Want To Know Some More About These Countries?

You could go to your library and ask to borrow some of these books.

"THIS IS OUR COUNTRY" SERIES

Children of the Highlands (Scotland)

Children of Olympus (Greece)

THE "LET'S VISIT" SERIES

Canada	Germany	Scotland
China	Greece	United States
Colombia	Ireland	West Africa

THE "LOOKING AT" SERIES

Greece	Denmark	Nigeria
Great Britain	Germany	China

"THIS IS" SERIES

London	New York	Edinburgh
Hong Kong	San Francisco	Munich
Ireland	Greece	Washington, D.C.

MY VILLAGE IN GREECE
MY VILLAGE IN IRELAND   by Sonia and Tim Gidal

The Philippines	Patricia K. Brooks
Land and Peoples of Nigeria	Brenda-Lu and Harrison Forman
Picture Story of Denmark	Hester O'Neill
Picture Story of the Philippines	Hester O'Neill
First Book of South America	William E. Carter
Picture Story of Britain	Noël Streatfeild

The Girl Guides of Canada/Guides du Canada are grateful to the many people who contributed to the development of the material contained in this book "Brownies Around the World, Book 2".

These include girls and their leaders, member countries of the World Association and members of the National Standing Committees.

Written by: Ismay McCarrick
Illustrator: Frances Shadbolt

Revised, 1979

 11